Coding in Scratch: Projects Workbook

Written by

Steve Setford
& Jon Woodcock

DK

DK | Penguin Random House

Written by
Steve Setford & Jon Woodcock
Editor Steve Setford
Designer Peter Radcliffe
US Editor Allison Singer
Publisher Sarah Larter
Art Director Martin Wilson
Jacket Designers Charlotte Jennings
Producer, Pre-Production Dragana Puvacic
Producer Priscilla Reby
Publishing Director Sophie Mitchell

First American Edition, 2016
Published in the United States by DK Publishing
345 Hudson Street, New York, New York 10014

Copyright © 2016 Dorling Kindersley Limited
DK, a Division of Penguin Random House LLC
16 17 18 19 20   10 9 8 7 6 5 4 3 2 1
001-285394-July/2016

A catalog record for this book
is available from the Library of Congress.
ISBN 978-1-4654-4402-8

DK books are available at special discounts when purchased in
bulk for sales promotions, premiums, fund-raising, or educational
use. For details, contact: DK Publishing Special Markets,
345 Hudson Street, New York, New York 10014
SpecialSales@dk.com

Printed and bound in China

Scratch is developed by the Lifelong Kindergarten group at
MIT Media Lab. See http://scratch.mit.edu

A WORLD OF IDEAS:
SEE ALL THERE IS TO KNOW

www.dk.com

Contents

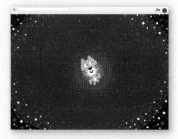

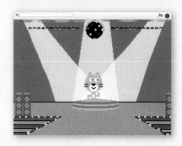

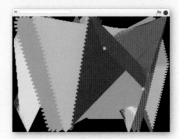

Hello, Scratch!

How do computers know what to do? For every task, they need to follow a detailed list of instructions called a program. Scratch makes it easy to create programs using ready-made blocks. Scratch puts you in control!

What's what in Scratch

In a typical Scratch project, programs called scripts control characters and objects known as sprites. The sprites appear in a part of the Scratch screen called the stage.

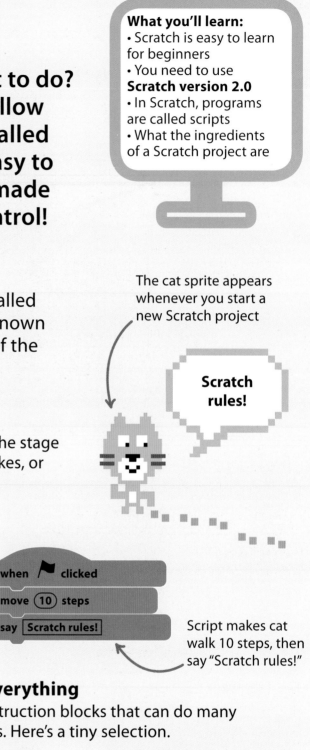

The cat sprite appears whenever you start a new Scratch project

Scratch rules!

Sprites

Sprites are things that can move around on the stage in a project. They may be animals, people, cakes, or even spaceships! Scripts bring sprites to life.

Scripts

Scripts are made of colored blocks that you drag with a computer mouse and put together like jigsaw pieces. Each block contains one instruction. Scratch reads through a script from top to bottom.

when 🏳 clicked
move (10) steps
say | Scratch rules! |

Script makes cat walk 10 steps, then say "Scratch rules!"

READ ME!

This book is based on **Scratch 2.0**, the latest version of Scratch at the time of writing. The projects won't work on older versions, so make sure you have 2.0. **See page 40 for details on how to get Scratch.**

Blocks for everything

Scratch has instruction blocks that can do many different things. Here's a tiny selection.

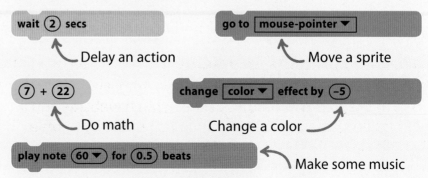

wait (2) secs
— Delay an action

go to | mouse-pointer ▼ |
— Move a sprite

(7) + (22)
— Do math

change | color ▼ | effect by (-5)
Change a color

play note (60 ▼) for (0.5) beats
Make some music

The stage

All the action in a Scratch project, such as this game, takes place on the stage. Sprites can move around on the stage, often in front of a background image called a "backdrop." Scratch measures distances on the stage in units called steps. The stage is 480 steps wide and 360 steps tall.

The red button stops all scripts

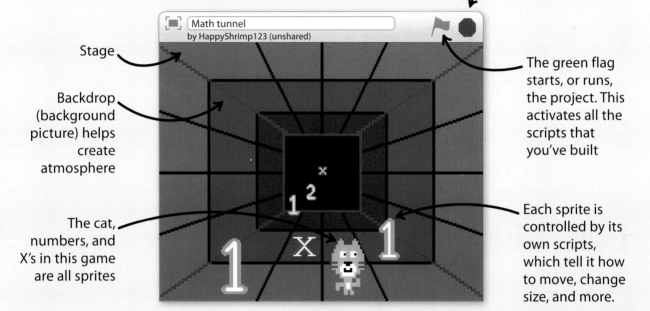

Stage

Backdrop (background picture) helps create atmosphere

The cat, numbers, and X's in this game are all sprites

The green flag starts, or runs, the project. This activates all the scripts that you've built

Each sprite is controlled by its own scripts, which tell it how to move, change size, and more.

Libraries

There are plenty of ready-made items to get you started in the Scratch libraries. These collections of sprites, backdrops, sounds and music clips can all be used in your own projects.

Right-clicking

Sometimes in Scratch you need to "right click" with the computer mouse. Don't worry if you only have one button on your mouse. Instead of right-clicking, you can usually hold down the control (CTRL/ctrl) or shift key as you click.

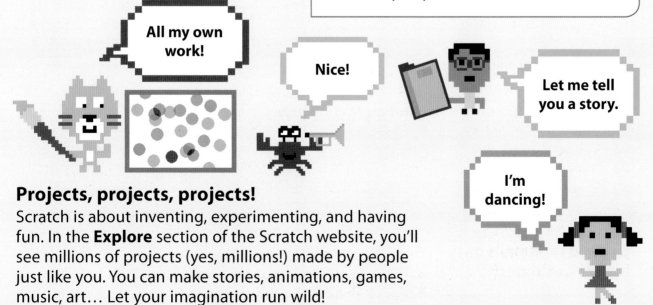

All my own work!

Nice!

Let me tell you a story.

I'm dancing!

Projects, projects, projects!

Scratch is about inventing, experimenting, and having fun. In the **Explore** section of the Scratch website, you'll see millions of projects (yes, millions!) made by people just like you. You can make stories, animations, games, music, art… Let your imagination run wild!

Exploring Scratch

When you open Scratch, this is what you'll see. It's called the Scratch editor, and it has all you need to create your projects. Take some time to explore it.

Experiment!
- Click the buttons and tabs to experiment
- Learn what each block color does
- Try building scripts

Type the name of your project here—this project is an animated story about a bear

Save projects here

Delete sprite or script

Help tool

Click here for full-screen view

Click these to start (run) and stop projects

When you run a Scratch project, you see the action happening on the stage

Once upon a time...

Click on a sprite on the stage or in the sprite list to select it

All the sprites in your project appear here

You can also select the stage and edit (change) its scripts, backdrops, and sounds

Buttons to add new backdrops (background pictures)

Buttons to add new sprites

A blue box appears around the sprite you have selected. Click on **(i)** for detailed sprite information

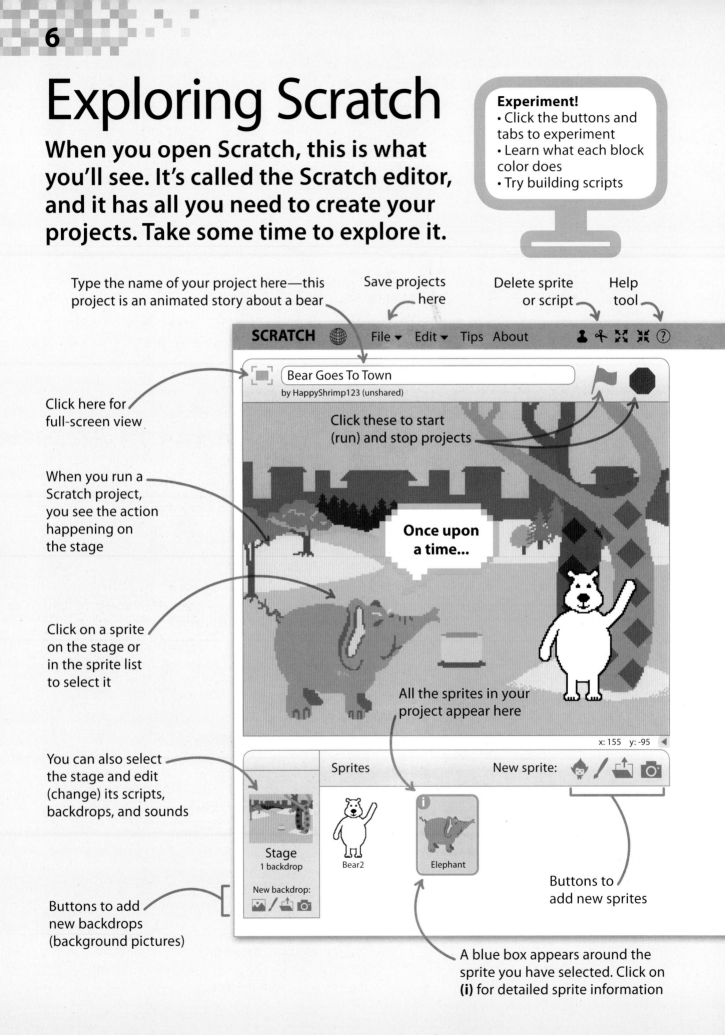

SCRATCH   File ▾ Edit ▾ Tips About

Bear Goes To Town
by HappyShrimp123 (unshared)

x: 155   y: -95

Sprites   New sprite:

Stage
1 backdrop
New backdrop:

Bear2   Elephant

▶ Map of the Scratch editor

The stage is where projects are run. A project's sprites are all shown in the sprite list. Script blocks can be found in the blocks palette. Build your scripts in the scripts area.

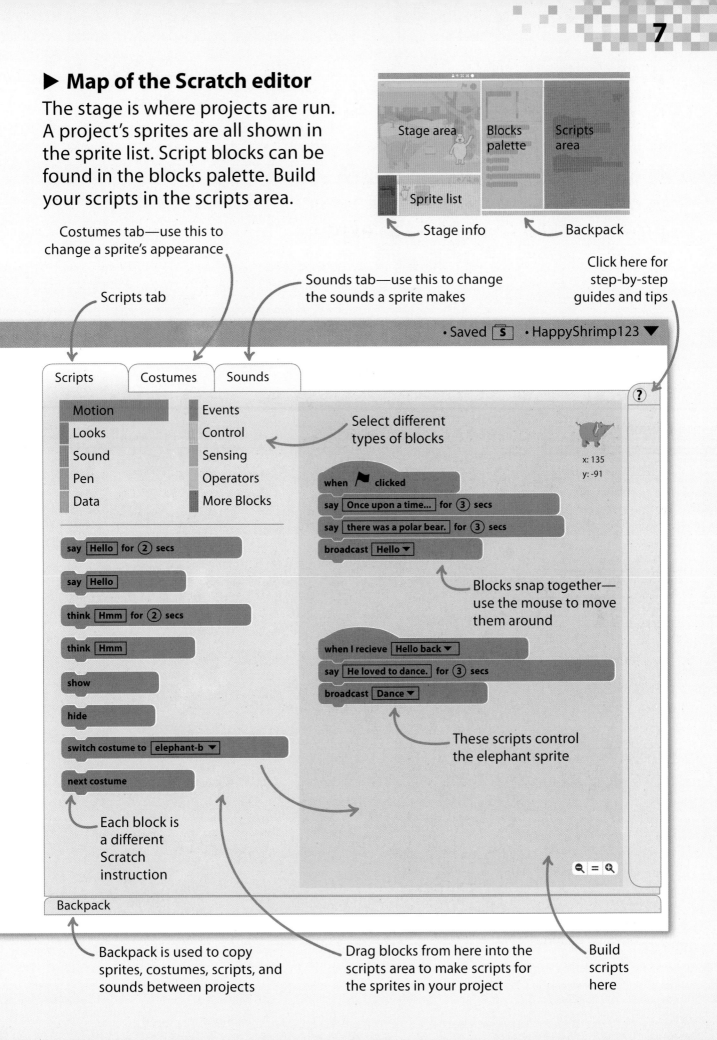

Stage area

Blocks palette

Scripts area

Sprite list

Stage info

Backpack

Costumes tab—use this to change a sprite's appearance

Scripts tab

Sounds tab—use this to change the sounds a sprite makes

Click here for step-by-step guides and tips

• Saved ⑤   • HappyShrimp123 ▼

Scripts   Costumes   Sounds

Motion
Looks
Sound
Pen
Data

Events
Control
Sensing
Operators
More Blocks

Select different types of blocks

when 🏴 clicked
say Once upon a time... for ③ secs
say there was a polar bear. for ③ secs
broadcast Hello ▼

x: 135
y: -91

Blocks snap together—use the mouse to move them around

say Hello for ② secs

say Hello

think Hmm for ② secs

think Hmm

show

hide

switch costume to elephant-b ▼

next costume

when I recieve Hello back ▼
say He loved to dance. for ③ secs
broadcast Dance ▼

These scripts control the elephant sprite

Each block is a different Scratch instruction

Backpack

Backpack is used to copy sprites, costumes, scripts, and sounds between projects

Drag blocks from here into the scripts area to make scripts for the sprites in your project

Build scripts here

Weird Music

Are you ready to build **Weird Music**, your first Scratch project? Don't worry, you won't have to do it all at once. Follow the numbered steps and put the project together piece by piece.

What you'll learn:
• How to build simple scripts to make a project
• How to control a sprite
• How to play music in Scratch
• How to make sprites change size and color

This readout shows the direction from the cat to the mouse-pointer

Type the name of your project here

Notes change according to where the mouse-pointer is on the stage

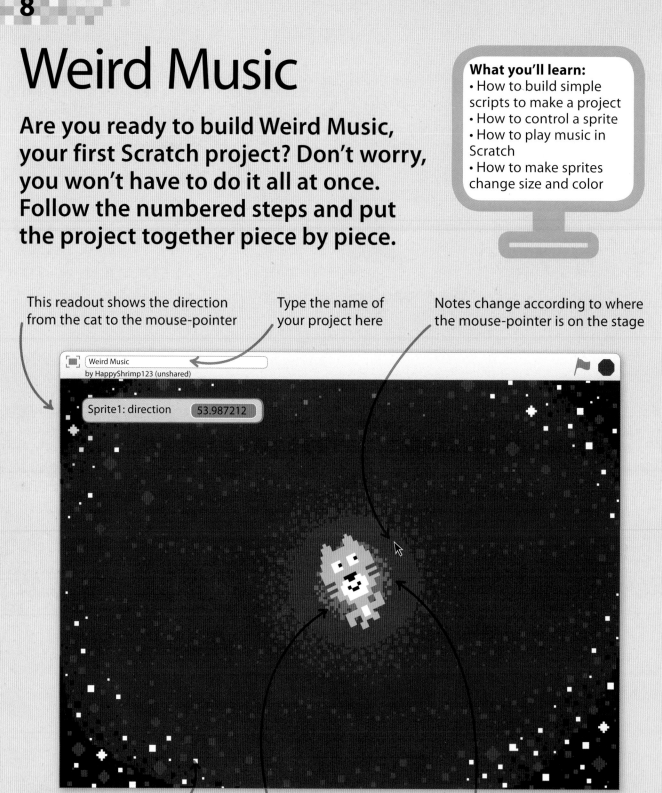

Weird Music
by HappyShrimp123 (unshared)

Sprite1: direction   53.987212

Colorful backdrop (this one's called "sparkling")

Scratch Cat shrinks, grows, and changes color

The cat always turns to face the mouse-pointer

▲ What you do

This project turns the stage into a strange musical instrument. Click with the mouse to play a note. Click on a different part of the stage and the note changes. All the while, Scratch Cat spins around in the center, changing color and size!

Get Scratch Cat spinning!

First, we'll make a script to control the cat. He'll remain in the center of the stage, but he won't stay still!

1 Open the Scratch editor: either choose **Create** on the Scratch website or click the Scratch symbol on your computer. Call your project "Weird Music."

2 Under the **Scripts** tab, look at the dark blue **Motion** section of the blocks palette. Click on the **point towards** block and drag it to the right into the scripts area. Select **mouse-pointer** from the drop-down menu.

3 Click the yellow **Control** section and select the **forever** block. Drag it over the **point towards** block, then let go. The blocks will lock together. Next, click the brown **Events** section. Drag the **when flag clicked** block to the top of the **forever** block.

4 Click the green flag at the top of the stage to start (run) the project. The cat should rotate so that he always faces the mouse-pointer. If he doesn't, check your script.

"forever" loops

Loops are sections of code that repeat again and again. A **forever** loop repeats the blocks inside it—forever! In your script to control the cat, the **forever** loop keeps the cat pointing at the mouse-pointer.

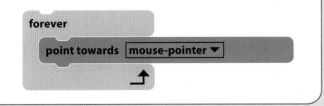

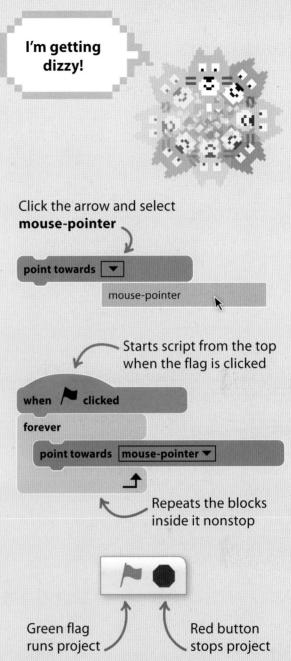

I'm getting dizzy!

Click the arrow and select **mouse-pointer**

point towards ▼

mouse-pointer

Starts script from the top when the flag is clicked

when ⚑ clicked

forever

point towards mouse-pointer ▼

Repeats the blocks inside it nonstop

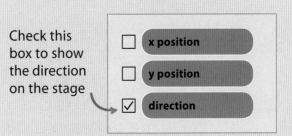

Green flag runs project

Red button stops project

5 Now go back to the **Motion** section. Click the small box next to the **direction** block. This will show the direction in which the cat is pointing on the stage.

Check this box to show the direction on the stage

☐ x position
☐ y position
☑ direction

Play a note

Next, we'll build a second script for Scratch Cat. This script will allow us to play notes on musical instruments.

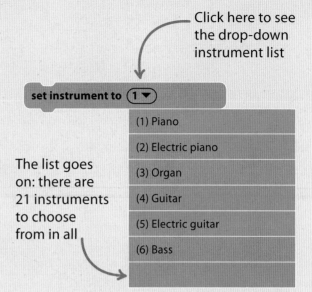

Click here to see the drop-down instrument list

set instrument to (1 ▼)

| (1) Piano |
| (2) Electric piano |
| (3) Organ |
| (4) Guitar |
| (5) Electric guitar |
| (6) Bass |

The list goes on: there are 21 instruments to choose from in all

6 Go to the pink **Sound** section and drag the **set instrument to** block into the cat's scripts area. This will be the first block of your second script. The arrow in the block's window lets you choose different instruments. Leave it set to **1** (the piano) for now.

7 Add this pink **play note** block from the **Sound** section to the bottom of the **set instrument to** block. It lets you choose which note to play and for how long. Keep it set to **note 60** and **0.5 beats**.

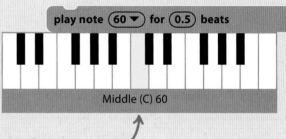

play note (60 ▼) for (0.5) beats

Middle (C) 60

Note 60 plays "Middle C"—the note in the center of a piano keyboard

8 Use your two pink blocks to build the second script shown here. You'll find the **wait until** block and the **forever** loop in the yellow **Control** section. The **mouse down?** block is in the light blue **Sensing** section.

when ⚑ clicked
forever
　wait until ⟨ mouse down? ⟩
　set instrument to (1 ▼)
　play note (60 ▼) for (0.5) beats

Nothing happens until the mouse is clicked down

Plays Middle C on the piano for half a beat

Who ever heard of a cat playing the piano?

9 Click the green flag to run the project. The piano should play a note when you click down with the mouse. If it doesn't, check that your script is correct. Experiment by playing different notes of different lengths, and see what other instruments sound like.

Make some music

Let's tweak the main script. The notes you play and their loudness (volume) will be controlled by the distance and direction from the cat to the mouse-pointer.

10 To understand how directions work on the stage, look at the picture below. Scratch describes the direction in which a sprite is facing in degrees (°), so our turtle is facing right (90°).

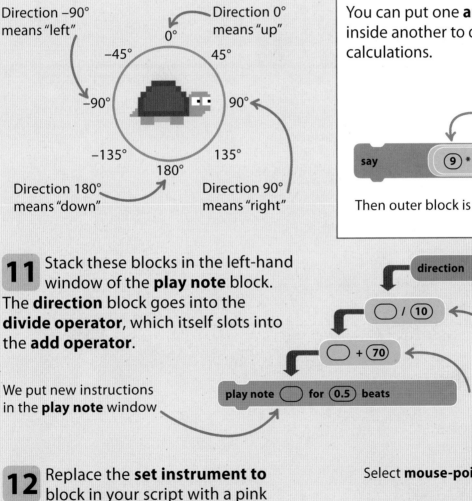

Direction –90° means "left"

Direction 0° means "up"

0°
−45°   45°
−90°   90°
−135°   135°
180°

Direction 180° means "down"

Direction 90° means "right"

Arithmetic operators

Four blocks in the green **Operators** section can do math with whatever numbers you type into them. You can also put variables and other blocks in their windows to do calculations.

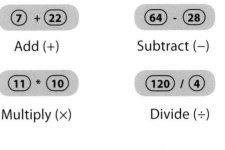

⑦ + ㉒
Add (+)

㉔ - ㉘
Subtract (−)

⑪ * ⑩
Multiply (×)

⑫⓪ / ④
Divide (÷)

You can put one **arithmetic operator** inside another to do more difficult calculations.

Inner block is worked out first

say (⑨ * ⑩) + ①

Then outer block is used

11 Stack these blocks in the left-hand window of the **play note** block. The **direction** block goes into the **divide operator**, which itself slots into the **add operator**.

We put new instructions in the **play note** window

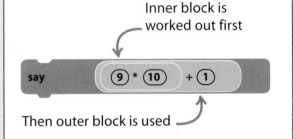

direction

From **Motion** section

◯ / ⑩

Type "10" here

◯ + ⑦⓪

Type "70" here

play note ◯ for ⓪.⑤ beats

12 Replace the **set instrument to** block in your script with a pink **set volume to** block. Stack these two blocks into its window, as shown here.

This block replaces the **set instrument to** block

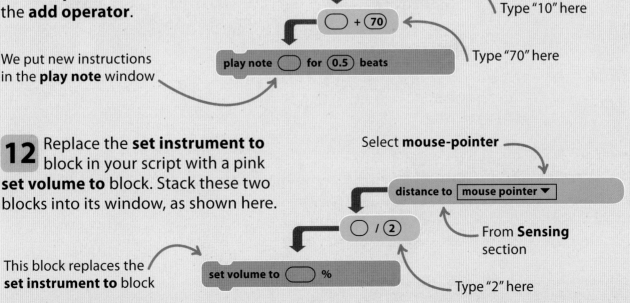

Select **mouse-pointer**

distance to [mouse pointer ▼]

From **Sensing** section

◯ / ②

set volume to ◯ %

Type "2" here

13 Your script should now look like this. Run the project. The notes you play will change as you move the mouse-pointer around the stage. They will also get louder farther away from the cat.

Point me at the cheese!

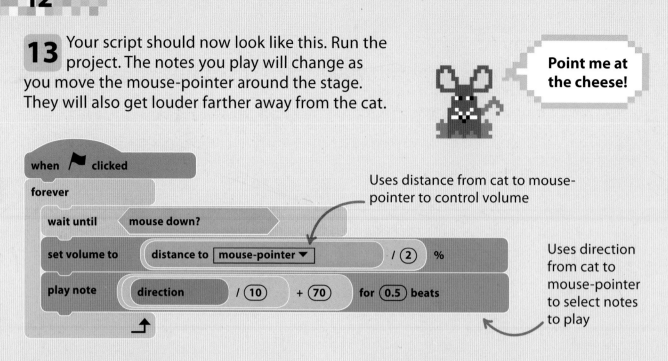

Uses distance from cat to mouse-pointer to control volume

Uses direction from cat to mouse-pointer to select notes to play

Finishing touches

Our final code tweaks will make Scratch Cat turn all the colors of the rainbow and shrink or grow in size as you play your crazy tunes.

14 Put the two blocks below into the **forever** loop, between the pink blocks. The **set size to** block enlarges or shrinks the cat as the volume changes. The set **color effect to** block changes his color as the mouse-pointer moves around the stage. Run the project and check that it works.

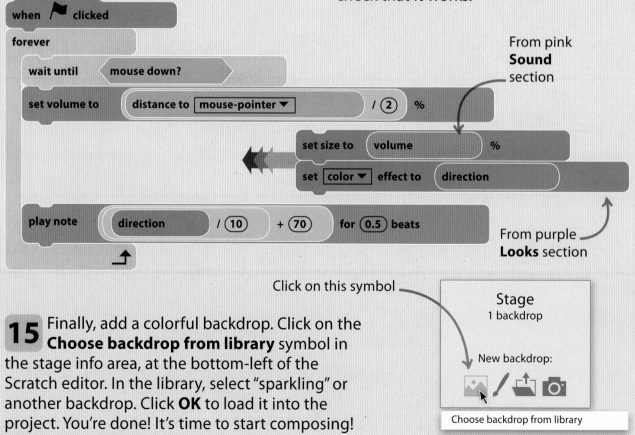

From pink **Sound** section

From purple **Looks** section

Click on this symbol

Stage
1 backdrop

New backdrop:

Choose backdrop from library

15 Finally, add a colorful backdrop. Click on the **Choose backdrop from library** symbol in the stage info area, at the bottom-left of the Scratch editor. In the library, select "sparkling" or another backdrop. Click **OK** to load it into the project. You're done! It's time to start composing!

Show what you know

You can make music, but can you make sense of these questions?

1. What color are the **Looks** blocks? ....

2. A .... repeats the blocks inside it endlessly.

3. Can you calculate the value of each block?

a. (17) + (2)   **b.** (9) - (4)   **c.** (3) * (4)   **d.** (15) / (3)

e. (8) + (2) * (3)   **f.** (3) + (8) * (2)

a. ....   **b.** ....   **c.** ....   **d.** ....

e. ....   **f.** ....

4. Draw a line from each turtle to the correct direction value.

90°   **180°**

−45°   **−135°**

5. Run the project and hold down the mouse button. What happens?

....

6. Go to the pink **Sound** blocks. Check the box beside the **volume** block.

What happens? ....

Check this box ⟶ ☑ | volume |

7. Can you figure out what this script does? Try adding it to the cat and

pressing the space bar as you play. ....

....

when | space ▼ | key pressed

set instrument to | pick random (1) to (21) |

Skywriting

In Skywriting, you'll use Scratch's **stamp** block, from the dark green **Pen** section, to spray patterns, messages, and pictures onto the stage. You can even make your own firework display!

What you'll learn:
• What variables are
• How **if-then** blocks work
• How to use the **stamp** and **clear** blocks
• How to make and use sliders for variables

Move this slider to make the spray broad or narrow

Low values on the **Width** slider narrow the spray so you can draw lines

Sky Writing
by HappyShrimp123 (unshared)

Width   10

Color   20

Move this slider to change the color of the splotches

High values on the **Width** slider spray the splotches over a wider area

Starry-sky backdrop

▲ What you do

Click down with the mouse to spray splotches of color onto the stage. Move the sliders to change the spray's spread and color. Hit the "c" key to clear the stage and start again.

Make a splotch!

The only sprite we need is a ball. We'll shrink it so that it looks like a tiny splotch of color. Then we can use it to create all sorts of shapes and patterns on the stage, and even to write.

See you later!

1 Start a new project. Call it "Skywriting." In the sprite list, right-click on the cat. Select **delete** from the pop-up menu. Good-bye, Scratch Cat!

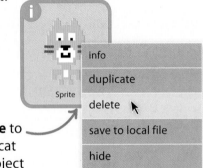

Select **delete** to remove the cat from the project

2 Click on the sprite symbol at the top of the sprite list to go to the library. Choose the "Ball" sprite and click **OK** to load it into your game.

Click the sprite symbol

New sprite:

Choose sprite from library

Ball

3 Next, build and run this script. Clicking the mouse "stamps" a splotch (a tiny image of the Ball sprite) onto the stage. Keep the mouse button pressed down to draw lines.

Change the number here from 100 to 10

Blocks inside run only when mouse button is pressed

```
when 🏴 clicked
set size to (10) %
forever
    if      mouse down?      then
        go to mouse-pointer ▼
        stamp
```

4 Now make the short script below. It erases all the splotches when you press "c."

```
when c ▼ key pressed
clear
```

Stamps an image of the sprite onto the stage

"if-then"

An **if-then** block wraps around other blocks and uses a "true or false?" question to control whether those blocks are run or skipped. When Scratch gets to an **if-then** block, it runs the blocks inside only if the answer to the question is true.

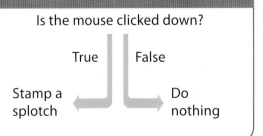

Is the mouse clicked down?

True   False

Stamp a splotch   Do nothing

5 In the orange **Data** section, click on **Make a Variable**. Type **"Width"** as the variable's name in the pop-up window and hit **OK**. When the block for the variable **Width** appears in the **Data** section, make sure the check box beside it is checked so it can be seen on the stage.

Variables

A variable is like a labeled box in which you can store data, such as words or numbers. The data stored in a variable is called its value. The variable you made has the label **Width**. The value it stores is the width of the splotch spray, measured in steps across the stage.

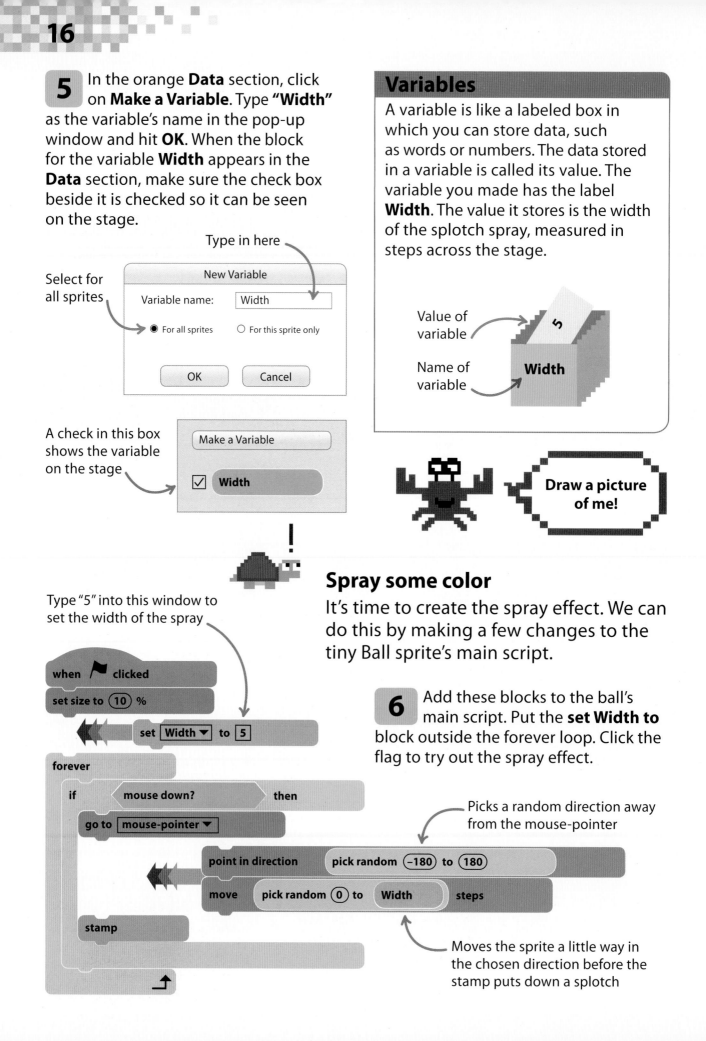

Type in here

Select for all sprites

New Variable

Variable name: Width

● For all sprites ○ For this sprite only

OK   Cancel

Value of variable

Name of variable **Width**

A check in this box shows the variable on the stage

Make a Variable

☑ **Width**

Draw a picture of me!

Spray some color

It's time to create the spray effect. We can do this by making a few changes to the tiny Ball sprite's main script.

Type "5" into this window to set the width of the spray

when 🏳 clicked

set size to (10) %

set Width ▼ to 5

forever

if mouse down? then

go to mouse-pointer ▼

point in direction pick random (-180) to (180)

move pick random (0) to Width steps

stamp

6 Add these blocks to the ball's main script. Put the **set Width to** block outside the forever loop. Click the flag to try out the spray effect.

Picks a random direction away from the mouse-pointer

Moves the sprite a little way in the chosen direction before the stamp puts down a splotch

7 Create a new variable called **"Color."** Make sure its check box is checked so the variable appears on the stage.

This box should be checked

Make a Variable
☑ **Color**

8 Add this block to the main script. It sets the color of the splotches to whatever you select with the **Color** slider. (We'll make the slider next.)

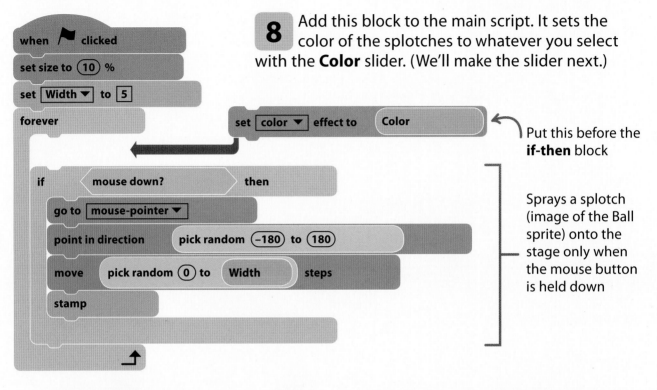

Put this before the **if-then** block

Sprays a splotch (image of the Ball sprite) onto the stage only when the mouse button is held down

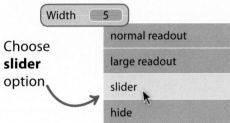

Choose **slider** option

normal readout
large readout
slider
hide

9 A slider lets you change a variable's value from the stage. Right-click on each readout and select **slider** from the pop-up menu. The **Color** slider alters the splotches' color. The **Width** slider makes them spread out or cluster together. Run the project and experiment with the sliders.

Slider Range
Min: 0
Max: 200
OK   Cancel

10 To ensure you have the greatest range of colors to use, right-click on the **Color** slider and select **set slider min and max**. Change the values in the **Slider Range** box to 0 (minimum) and 200 (maximum), then click **OK**.

11 Lastly, go to the stage info area, at the bottom-left of the Scratch editor. Click on the **Choose backdrop from library** symbol. Select "stars" in the library and hit **OK**. Now you're all set to make it a colorful night! Happy skywriting!

Click here for the backdrop library

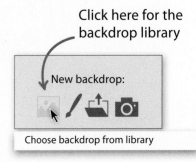

Show what you know
Can you write the right answers to these puzzling problems?

1. What is a variable? ....

2. In which section do you find the variable blocks? ....

3. Why do you check the box next to a variable? ....
....

4. What does a slider do? ....
....

5. In which section do you find **stamp** and **clear**? ....
....

6. What is the **stamp** block for? ....

7. What is the **clear** block for? ....

8. In an **if-then** block there is a question at the top and some blocks inside. Use these words to complete the sentences below: **skips**   **runs**

    a. If the answer to the question is true (yes), then Scratch
    .... the blocks inside the **if-then** block.

    b. If the answer to the question is false (no), then Scratch
    .... the blocks inside the **if-then** block.

9. If you added the script below to the Ball sprite, what would pressing the space bar do? ....

when [space ▼] key pressed
set [color] to (pick random (0) to (200))

Try it out in Scratch to see if you're right

10. The range of the **Width** slider goes from 0 to 100. This leads to very spread-out paint. Can you describe the steps to change the range to **0 to 30** and make the splotches closer together?

    a. ....

    b. ....

    c. ....

    d. ....

Quiz Time!

Scratch Cat knows his times tables—but do you? In this tricky quiz, he fires questions at you from a glamorous, spotlit stage. Click the green flag to see if you can handle the pressure!

What you'll learn:
- How to ask questions and handle answers
- Advanced block stacking
- How to use **join** blocks to link words or variables
- How an **if-then-else** block works

This background is called "spotlight-stage"

Questions appear in a speech bubble

Use the green flag and red button to start and stop the quiz

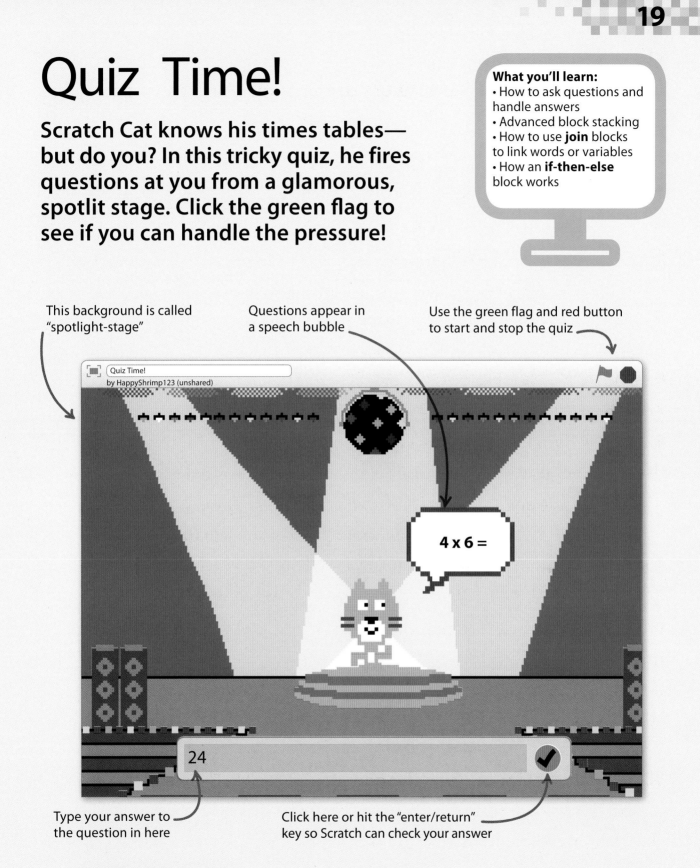

Type your answer to the question in here

Click here or hit the "enter/return" key so Scratch can check your answer

▲ What you do

Scratch Cat will ask you ten fiendish questions about your 1 to 12 times tables. Type your answers into the bar at the bottom of the stage for him to check. You score a point for each answer you get right. Test yourself: can you get ten out of ten?

A script for Quizmaster Scratch Cat

This project has only one script. It's a long, complicated script, and you can't try out the project until the script is complete. But it contains everything Scratch Cat needs to quiz you and keep track of the score.

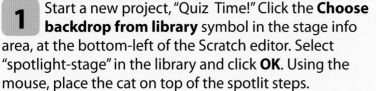

The spotlight's on me!

1 Start a new project, "Quiz Time!" Click the **Choose backdrop from library** symbol in the stage info area, at the bottom-left of the Scratch editor. Select "spotlight-stage" in the library and click **OK**. Using the mouse, place the cat on top of the spotlit steps.

Click here to open the backdrop library

New backdrop:

Choose backdrop from library

2 Click on the cat sprite below the stage, then click on the **Scripts** tab. Before we build any code, we need to create four variables. Call them **"Number1,"** **"Number2," "CorrectAnswer,"** and **"Score."** Uncheck their check boxes so they don't appear on the stage.

☐ Number1

☐ Number2

☐ CorrectAnswer

☐ Score

Make sure there are no checks in these boxes

3 Put this group of blocks together to build the first part of the script. It randomly selects two numbers from 1 to 12 to multiply together. Then it works out the correct answer.

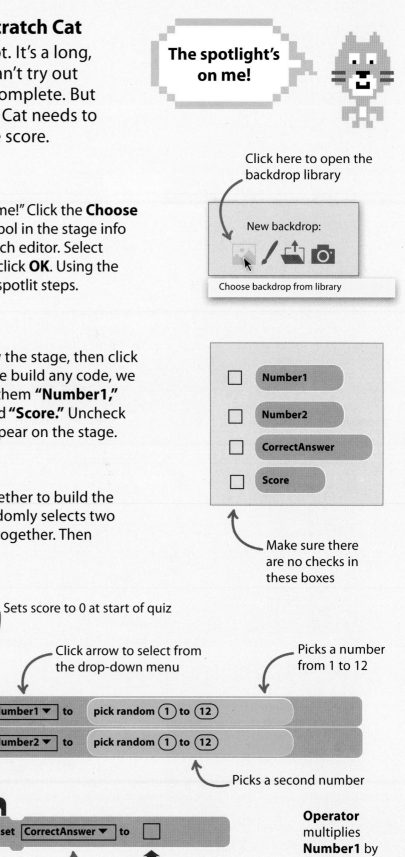

Sets score to 0 at start of quiz

Click arrow to select from the drop-down menu

Picks a number from 1 to 12

```
when [flag] clicked
set Score ▼ to 0
repeat 10
```

```
set Number1 ▼ to   pick random 1 to 12
set Number2 ▼ to   pick random 1 to 12
```

Picks a second number

Operator multiplies **Number1** by **Number2**

```
set CorrectAnswer ▼ to ☐
```

This **repeat** loop runs the blocks inside it ten times and then stops

Stores answer in **CorrectAnswer** variable

◯ * ◯

Number1   Number2

"join"

The green **join** block from the **Operators** section links two values together and reports the result, such as joining words and variables to form a sentence.

join | hello | world

4 Now create this stack of blocks. It takes the numbers stored in the variables and uses them to ask a multiplication question.

ask [ ] and wait

Type "=" in here

join [ ] [=]

Number2

The **join** blocks put the question together

join [ ] [ ]

Stores number picked by **set Number1 to** block

join [ ] [×]

Number1

Type "x" in here

5 Next, make this stack of blocks. It will make Scratch Cat tell you your score out of ten at the end of the quiz.

say [ ]

join | You scored | [ ]

Type "/10" in here

Type "You scored " here (add a space after "scored")

Puts together your score out of ten

join [ ] | /10 |

Score

Uses the number stored in the variable **Score**

I love those stacking blocks!

6 Insert the **ask** block into the **repeat** loop, after the three **set to** blocks. Then add the **say** block at the end of the script, outside the loop.

when ⚑ clicked

repeat (10)

set [Number1 ▼] to (pick random (1) to (12))

set [Number2 ▼] to (pick random (1) to (12))

set [CorrectAnswer ▼] to (Number1 * Number2)

ask (join (join (join (Number1) [×] (Number2)) [=])) and wait

Asks you a question and waits for you to type in the answer

Announces your score after ten questions have been asked

say (join | You scored | (join (Score) | /10 |))

7 You also need to make this section of code. Put it in the **repeat** loop, after the **ask** block. If you type in the right answer, the cat says "Correct!" and a point is added to your score. If not, the cat says "Wrong!" and tells you the correct answer.

"if-then-else"

An **if-then-else** block is a bit like an **if-then** block, but it holds two sets of blocks. It asks a question and runs one set of blocks if the answer is "yes." It runs the other set of blocks if the answer is "no."

This **answer** block stores what you type

```
if       answer  =  CorrectAnswer       then
    change Score ▼ by ①
    say Correct! for ① secs
else
    say Join Wrong! Answer is    CorrectAnswer    for ② secs
```

Type "Correct!" into this block's window

Answer shows on the stage for 2 seconds

Type "Wrong! Answer is " here (include a space after "is")

8 Your script is now complete and should look like this. Run it—does it work OK? If it doesn't, check that you have all the correct blocks in the correct order. Challenge your friends to see who's the multiplication master!

```
when ⚑ clicked
set Score ▼ to ⓪
repeat ⑩
    set Number1 ▼ to    pick random ① to ⑫
    set Number2 ▼ to    pick random ① to ⑫
    set CorrectAnswer ▼ to    Number1 * Number2
    ask    join join join Number1 × Number2 = and wait
    if       answer  =  CorrectAnswer       then
        change Score by ①
        say Correct! for ① secs
    else
        say Join Wrong! Answer is    CorrectAnswer    for ② secs
say    join You scored    join Score    /10
```

Sets a question and works out the answer

Asks the question

Responds to the answer you type in

Checks to see if the answer's correct

Tells you your score

Race you to the next project!

Show what you know
Think you're a quiz expert? Then see how you do with this one!

1. Can you match these Scratch **Operator** blocks to the calculations they show? Draw a line from each block to the correct word.

| 15 / 3 | 3 * 4 | 17 + 2 | 9 - 4 |

a. Add   **b.** Subtract   **c.** Divide   **d.** Multiply

2. How could you make the quiz questions go all the way up to **20 × 20**?

....

3. How could you stop the easy **1 ×** or **× 1** questions from appearing?

....

4. How could you increase the number of questions in the quiz to **20**?

....

....

5. When you reply to a question in an **ask** block, where does Scratch store what you type in? ....

6. Where could you put these blocks in the code opposite to play a high note for a correct answer and a low note for an incorrect answer?

a. `play note (90 ▼) for (0.5) beats`   **b.** `play note (20 ▼) for (1.0) beats`

a. ....

b. ....

7. Can you draw arrows to show where each bit of code should go to make Scratch Cat greet you with your name?

`when ⚑ clicked`   `join [  ] [  ]`   **Hello**

`ask [What's your name] and wait`   `say [  ]`   **answer**

Pet Party

Give your pet a makeover with this crazy project! Pet Party is a ton of fun, and it teaches you some useful new Scratch skills—especially how to make your own sprites.

What you'll learn:
• How to draw sprites using the paint editor
• How to load your own images into a project
• How to use message blocks to trigger scripts
• How to load sounds

Get your pet in the party mood by dragging a colorful hat onto his head!

The eyes swivel to point toward the mouse-pointer

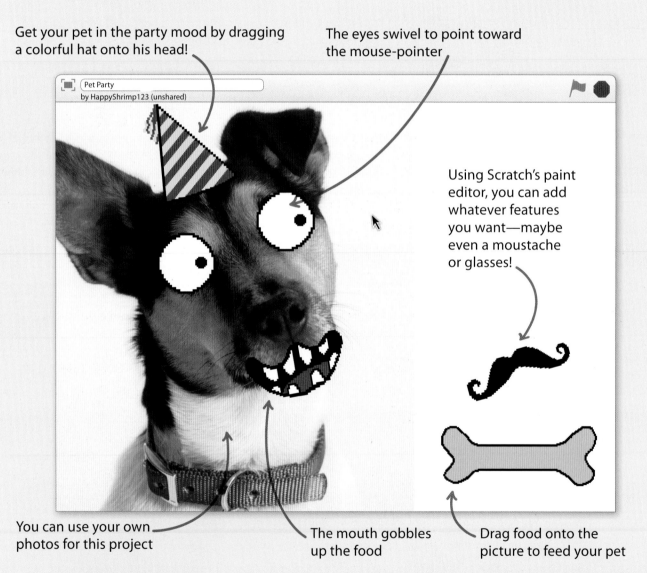

Using Scratch's paint editor, you can add whatever features you want—maybe even a moustache or glasses!

You can use your own photos for this project

The mouth gobbles up the food

Drag food onto the picture to feed your pet

▲ What you do

In this project, you'll draw sprites and use them to add funny features, such as swiveling eyes and a silly party hat, to a photo of a pet or other animal. You'll also be able to feed your pet and watch it gulp down food noisily!

Make some funny features

Let's start by giving your pet some big, googly eyes and a fancy party hat to wear.

1 First, take a photo of your pet using a camera or a phone. Make it a portrait (upright) photo, not a landscape (horizontal) one. Upload the photo from your camera or phone to your computer. You may need to ask a parent to help you.

Portrait

Use a portrait picture, please!

Landscape

2 Start a new Scratch project called "Pet Party." Go to the sprite list and delete Scratch Cat. Then click on **Upload sprite from file** (the file symbol). Select the picture of your pet and click **OK**. Your pet will appear in the sprite list.

Click the file symbol

New sprite:

Upload sprite from file

3 If your photo title is just a number, you'll need to rename your pet sprite. Select it and click on the blue **(i)** in its top corner. Type your pet's name into the window of the sprite's information panel.

Click here

Type in this window

20176.jpeg

Scruff

x: 84   y: -69   direction: –90°
rotation style:
can drag in player: ☐
show: ☑

4 Using the mouse, click and drag the photo to the left-hand side of the stage. Leave room on the right for the bone and the hat.

5 To draw the eyes, first click on **Paint new sprite** (the paintbrush symbol) at the top of the sprite list to open the paint editor.

Picture problems

If you don't have a pet or you don't have a camera or a phone to take a photo, ask a parent to help you find a copyright-free animal photo on the Internet that's in the public domain. Alternatively, you can draw or trace a picture of an animal, scan it, and save it on your computer.

Click here to draw a new sprite

New sprite:

Paint new sprite

These new eyes are fantastic!

6 Check that **Bitmap Mode** is selected in the bottom-right corner of the paint editor (see below), and that black is selected on the color palette.

7 Next, click the circle tool on the left-hand side of the paint editor. Make sure the outline shape (rather than solid color) is selected in the bottom-left corner.

Circle tool

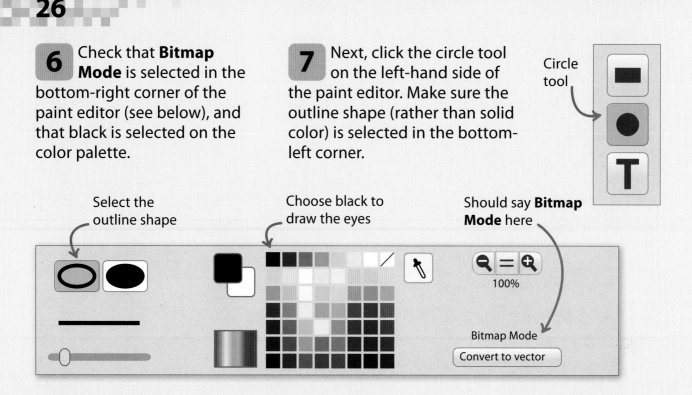

Select the outline shape

Choose black to draw the eyes

Should say **Bitmap Mode** here

100%

Bitmap Mode

Convert to vector

8 While holding down the shift key, click and drag the mouse to draw a circle. Select the **Fill with color** tool (the paint pot) and choose white on the color palette. Click on the eye to make it white. To add a pupil, select the circle tool, the solid-color shape, and black on the palette. Draw a small circle inside the eye, close to the edge, in the "3 o'clock" position.

Fill with color tool

Draw the pupil at "3 o'clock"

Fill the eye with white

9 To make the eye turn properly, you need to center it. Select the **Set costume center** tool (in the top-right corner of the paint editor), then click in the very center of the eye.

Set costume center tool

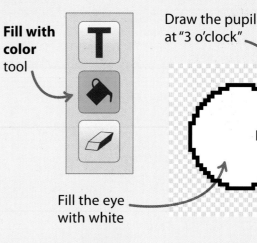

Click in the center of the eye sprite

when ⚑ clicked
forever
   go to front
   point towards mouse-pointer ▼

Shows the eye sprite in front of the photo

Makes the eye swivel to "look" at the mouse-pointer

10 Add this script to the eye sprite. It tells the eye to point at the mouse-pointer, wherever the mouse-pointer is on the stage.

11 Right-click the eye sprite and select **duplicate** from the drop-down menu that appears. This will make a copy of the eye and its script.

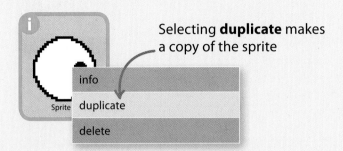

Selecting **duplicate** makes a copy of the sprite

info
duplicate
delete

13 Now click the flag to run the eye scripts. Both eyes should swivel to follow the mouse-pointer as you move it around the stage.

Pet Party
by HappyShrimp123 (unshared)

If the eyes don't swivel, check your script

15 In the sprite list, select the hat and click on the blue **(i)** in its top corner. Rename the sprite "Hat." Check the **can drag in player** box in the information panel, so you can drag the hat onto your pet's head.

Sends the hat to the right-hand side of the stage

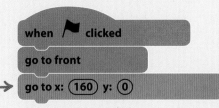

when 🏳 clicked
go to front
go to x: (160) y: (0)

12 Click and drag the eyes into position on the picture. If you're not happy with their size, use the **Grow** and **Shrink** tools on the bar along the top of the Scratch editor to make them bigger or smaller.

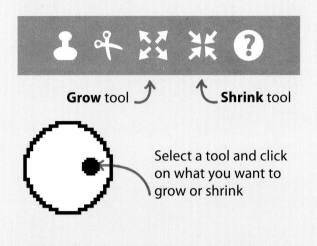

Grow tool   **Shrink** tool

Select a tool and click on what you want to grow or shrink

14 Open the paint editor again by clicking on **Paint new sprite** (the paintbrush). Make another new sprite—the hat. When you've finished, center your sprite (see step 9).

Use the **Brush** tool to make tassels

Use the **Line** tool to make stripes

Use the paint pot to fill in colors

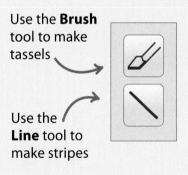

Hat
x: 84   y: -69   direction: −90° ⊖
rotation style: ↻ ↔ •
can drag in player: ☑
show: ☑

Checking here lets you drag the hat around in full-screen mode

16 Give the hat this code. The numbers, or coordinates, tell the hat where to appear on the stage at the start. Click the flag to try it out.

It's feeding time!

Your pet's tummy is rumbling. You'll need to draw some food for it to eat and a mouth so that your pet can gobble up the food with a "chomp!"

17 Click on **Paint new sprite** again to draw a food sprite. It could be a bone for a dog, a carrot for a horse, or lettuce for a rabbit. Center the sprite (see step 9), then rename it.

Draw an outline with the **Brush** tool, then fill it with color

18 Drag the brown **broadcast and wait** block into the food sprite's scripts area. Click on the arrow in the window and select **new message** from the drop-down menu. Then type "Eat" into the pop-up box. Click **OK**.

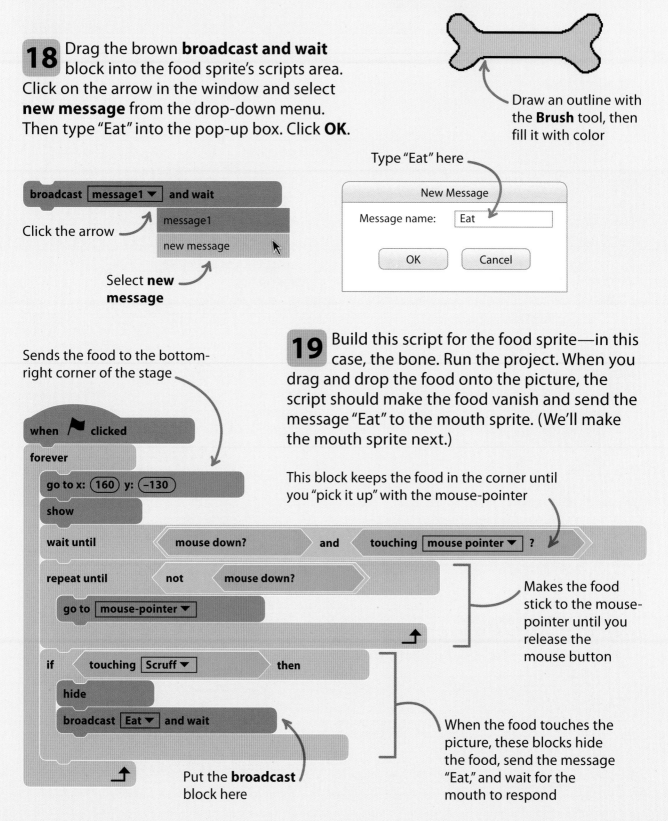

broadcast [message1 ▼] and wait

Click the arrow →

message1

new message

Select **new message**

Type "Eat" here

New Message

Message name: [Eat]

OK   Cancel

Sends the food to the bottom-right corner of the stage

when ⚑ clicked

forever

go to x: (160) y: (−130)

show

wait until ⟨ ⟨mouse down?⟩ and ⟨touching [mouse pointer ▼] ?⟩ ⟩

repeat until ⟨ not ⟨mouse down?⟩ ⟩

go to [mouse-pointer ▼]

if ⟨ touching [Scruff ▼] ⟩ then

hide

broadcast [Eat ▼] and wait

Put the **broadcast** block here

19 Build this script for the food sprite—in this case, the bone. Run the project. When you drag and drop the food onto the picture, the script should make the food vanish and send the message "Eat" to the mouth sprite. (We'll make the mouth sprite next.)

This block keeps the food in the corner until you "pick it up" with the mouse-pointer

Makes the food stick to the mouse-pointer until you release the mouse button

When the food touches the picture, these blocks hide the food, send the message "Eat," and wait for the mouth to respond

20 Now draw another new sprite—your pet's mouth. The sprite can be just a mouth shape. If you're skilled at drawing sprites, you can try adding teeth and a tongue. Rename the sprite and drag it into position on the picture.

Rename your sprite when it appears in the sprite list

Mouth

21 Let's add an eating sound to the mouth. With the mouth selected, go to the **Sounds** tab and click **Choose sound from library** (the speaker symbol). In the library, select "chomp" and then hit **OK**.

You've got great teeth!

Clicking on the speaker under the **Sounds** tab will take you to the sound library

Choose sound from library

22 Build this code for the mouth. When the script receives the message "Eat," it plays the sound of eating and makes the mouth look as though it's swallowing the food, which disappears. Congratulations—you've completed Pet Party! Click the flag to try it out. Why not make your own funny features to add to the project?

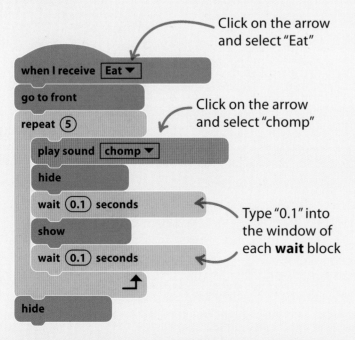

Click on the arrow and select "Eat"

Click on the arrow and select "chomp"

Type "0.1" into the window of each **wait** block

Messages

Scratch sprites can use messages to "talk" to each other.

```
broadcast Eat ▼
```

This block broadcasts (sends out) a message that tells other sprites to do something.

```
broadcast Eat ▼ and wait
```

This block tells other sprites to do something but waits until they finish before continuing.

```
when I receive Eat ▼
```

This block runs any script below it when it receives a particular broadcast message.

Show what you know
Your pet is ready to party—but are *you* ready to take this test?

1. The **when I receive** block will only run the script below it when it gets a message from a .... block.

2. The .... is where you draw new sprites.

3. You can resize sprites using the .... and .... tools.

4. Which block makes a sprite disappear from the stage? ....

5. If you draw your eye like this in the paint editor, what will happen when you run its script? Try your ideas out in Scratch.

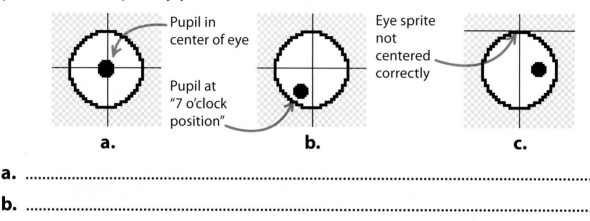

Pupil in center of eye

Pupil at "7 o'clock position"

Eye sprite not centered correctly

a.   **b.**   **c.**

a. ....

b. ....

c. ....

6. You used coordinates in the **go to x: y:** block of the hat's script to position the hat on the stage. Draw lines to link these hats with their coordinates.

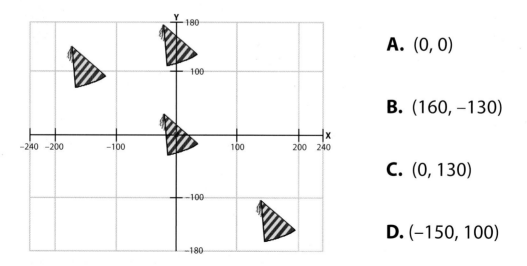

A. (0, 0)

B. (160, −130)

C. (0, 130)

D. (−150, 100)

7. How would you make a short script to add to Scruff the dog sprite so that he barks when he's clicked on?

Bounce Painting

Scratch has a magic pen that can draw lines wherever a sprite goes. In this project, you'll create two balls that bounce around the stage drawing beautiful, changing patterns.

What you'll learn:
• That Scratch has a pen that can draw lines when a sprite moves
• That local variables let identical copies of sprites store different data

This project looks great full-screen!

The two balls bounce around the stage

Each time the balls move a step, a colored line is drawn between them

Bounce Painting
by HappyShrimp123 (unshared)

The line changes color each time to create multicolored patterns

A dark or black background shows the patterns best

▲ What you do

You simply click the green flag to set the balls in motion. They always set off with a random speed and direction, so you never get the same pattern twice. After a while, the screen fills up, so the project has a script to clear the stage.

Get the balls bouncing!

We'll start by getting the balls bouncing around the stage. They won't paint any patterns just yet— we'll sort that out later.

1 Start a new project called "Bounce Painting." Delete the cat sprite, then load the sprite "Ball" from the library.

Ball

2 Go to the orange **Data** blocks and click on **Make a variable**. Type "Speed" in the pop-up window. Select **For this sprite only**, then click **OK**. When it appears in the **Data** section, uncheck its check box so it doesn't show on the stage.

New Variable
Variable name: **Speed**
○ For all sprites   ● For this sprite only
OK   Cancel

Click this option

3 Make this script for the ball. Click on the **broadcast** block's arrow and select **new message**. Type "Go" into the pop-up window and click **OK**.

when ⚑ clicked
broadcast Go ▼

Tells the **when I receive** block to run its script

Click here and select "Go"

Shrinks size of ball

Sets a random variable speed for just this sprite

when I receive Go ▼
set size to 20 %
set Speed ▼ to pick random 1 to 15
point in direction: pick random -180 to 180
forever
  move Speed steps
  if on edge, bounce

4 Now build this second script for the ball. It is triggered by the message "Go" and sets the ball bouncing nonstop.

Picks a random direction

Keeps the ball bouncing

5 Right-click on the ball and select **duplicate** to create Ball2. Run the project a few times. You'll notice that the balls always set off randomly, showing that each ball has its own version of the variable "Speed."

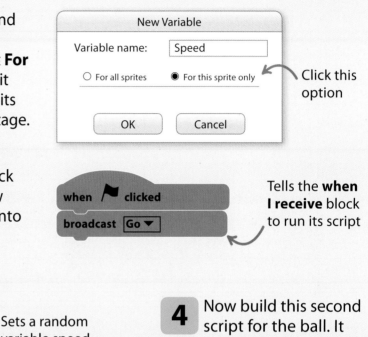

Ball

info
duplicate
delete
save to local file
hide

Local variables

When you create a variable for just one sprite and then copy the sprite, each sprite gets its own version of the variable. The two versions can be different, allowing the balls to go at different speeds. Programmers call this a "local variable."

Drawing lines, tidying up

The next task is to draw the colored line between the balls. Then we'll darken the backdrop. Finally, we'll make a script to clear the stage when it gets full.

6 Click on **Paint new sprite** to create a new, empty sprite that will draw the line. Call it "Line Draw." We don't need to see this sprite, so we won't draw a costume!

The new sprite doesn't need a costume

Line Draw

7 Add this script to the Line Draw sprite. It draws a colored line between the two balls, but it also changes the line's color a little each time. Run the project to test it.

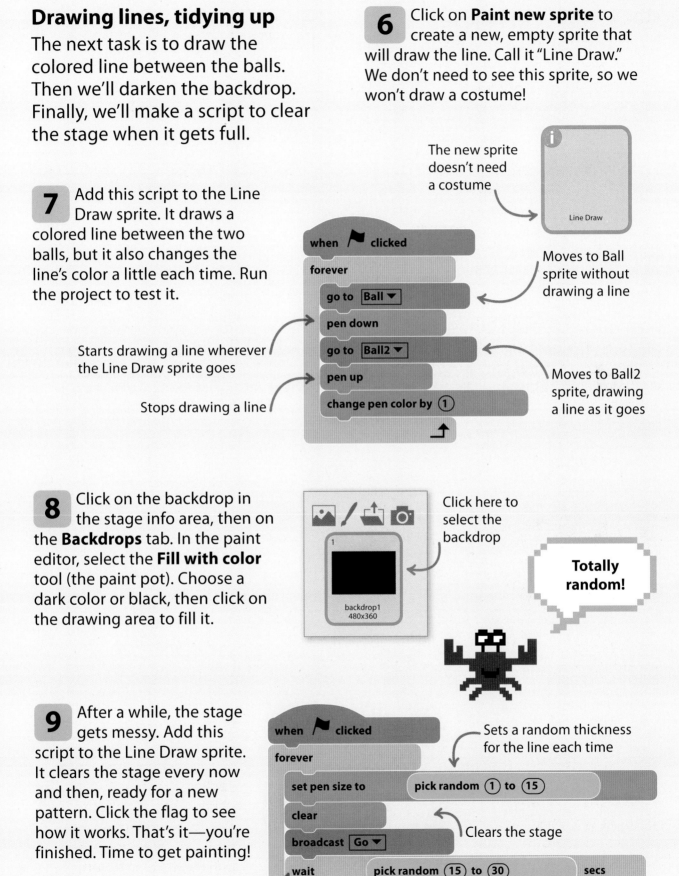

Moves to Ball sprite without drawing a line

```
when [flag] clicked
forever
    go to [Ball ▼]
    pen down
    go to [Ball2 ▼]
    pen up
    change pen color by (1)
```

Starts drawing a line wherever the Line Draw sprite goes

Stops drawing a line

Moves to Ball2 sprite, drawing a line as it goes

8 Click on the backdrop in the stage info area, then on the **Backdrops** tab. In the paint editor, select the **Fill with color** tool (the paint pot). Choose a dark color or black, then click on the drawing area to fill it.

Click here to select the backdrop

backdrop1
480x360

Totally random!

9 After a while, the stage gets messy. Add this script to the Line Draw sprite. It clears the stage every now and then, ready for a new pattern. Click the flag to see how it works. That's it—you're finished. Time to get painting!

```
when [flag] clicked
forever
    set pen size to (pick random (1) to (15))
    clear
    broadcast [Go ▼]
    wait (pick random (15) to (30)) secs
```

Sets a random thickness for the line each time

Clears the stage

Resets the drawing every 15 to 30 seconds

Show what you know

Get your brain cells bouncing with these tricky questions!

1. Draw a line to link each pen block to its correct meaning.

pen down   Clear all pen drawing off the stage

pen up   Start drawing as the sprite moves

set pen size to ③   Stop drawing as the sprite moves

clear   Set how wide the pen line is

2. What would the sprite be called if we duplicated Ball2? ....

3. With three balls, where would you put these two **go to** blocks into the script below to make it draw triangles instead of lines?

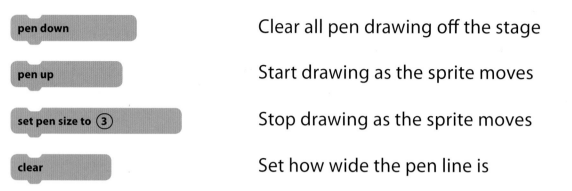

Draw an arrow to show where these blocks should go (hint: keep them together as a pair)

4. How would you get the lines to change color ten times quicker?

....

5. What happens if you add a **change shade by 10** pen block into the script below the **change pen color** block? ....

....

6. Select each ball sprite one by one, go to the **Data** section, and check the check box of its speed variable. Run the project. What do you notice?

....

....

Solutions

Well done. You've completed all the tasks! Time to check your "Show what you know" answers. How did you do? Are you a Scratch project expert now?

We know all the answers!

pages 8–13 Weird Music

1. The **Looks** blocks are **Purple**.

2. A **forever loop** repeats the blocks inside it endlessly.

3.

(17) + (2)
a. 19

(9) - (4)
b. 5

(3) * (4)
c. 12

(15) / (3)
d. 5

((8) + (2)) * (3)
e. 30

(3) + ((8) * (2))
f. 19

(For parts **e** and **f**, remember to calculate the inner block first, then use the result to calculate the outer block.)

4.

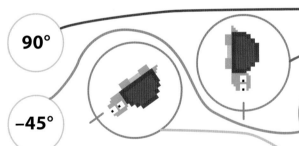

90°
−45°

180°
−135°

5. When you hold down the mouse button, Scratch plays a stream of notes. It stops only when you release the mouse button.

6. When you check the box beside the **volume** block under the **Sounds** tab, a readout for the volume setting appears on the stage.

7. The script picks a random musical instrument each time you press the space bar.

pages 14–18 Skywriting

1. A variable is used to store data in a program.

2. The variable blocks are found in the orange **Data** section, under the **Scripts** tab.

3. You check the box next to a variable to show the variable's name and value on the stage.

4. A slider lets you change the value of a variable from the stage.

5. You'll find the **stamp** and **clear** blocks in the dark green **Pen** section.

6. The **stamp** block leaves an image of a sprite on the stage.

7. The **clear** block removes all the stamps from the stage.

8a. If the answer to the question is true (yes), then Scratch **runs** the blocks inside the **if-then** block.

8b. If the answer to the question is false (no), then Scratch **skips** the blocks inside the **if-then** block.

9. If you add the script to the Ball sprite, Scratch chooses a random color for the splotches when you press the space bar. If you keep the space bar *and* the mouse key pressed down at the same time, you get a continuous spray of splotches that constantly change color!

10. To change the range of the **Width** slider from **0 to 30** and make the splotches closer together, you:

a. Right-click on the **Width** slider.

b. Select **set slider min and max**.

c. Type 30 into the **Max** window of the pop-up box.

d. Click **OK**.

Right click, then select **set slider min and max**

Width	5

normal readout

large readout

slider

set slider min and max

hide

Type **30** in here

Slider Range

Min: 0

Max: 30

OK   Cancel

pages 19–23 Quiz Time!

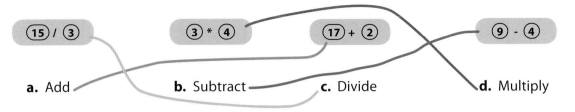

a. Add   b. Subtract   c. Divide   d. Multiply

2. To make the quiz questions go all the way up to **20 × 20**, change the upper limit in each **pick random** block to **20**.

3. To stop the easy **1 ×** or **× 1** questions, change the lower limit in each **pick random** block to **2**.

4. To increase the number of questions in the quiz to **20**, change the 10 at the top of the **repeat** loop to **20**, and the 1/10 in the last **say** block to **1/20**.

5. When you reply to a question in an **ask** block, Scratch stores what you type in an **answer** block.

6a. Make **a** the first block in the **if-then** part of the **if-then-else** block.

6b. Make **b** the first block in the **else** part of the **if-then-else** block.

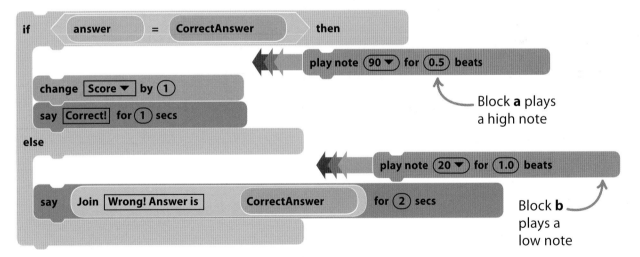

7. This is how you put the blocks together. Try building the script yourself.

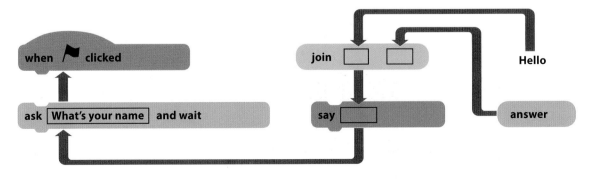

pages 24–30 Pet Party

1. The **when I receive** block will only run the script below it when it gets a message from a **broadcast** block.

2. The **paint editor** is where you draw new sprites.

3. You can resize sprites using the **grow** and **shrink** tools.

4. The **hide** block makes a sprite disappear from the stage.

5a. If you draw the pupil in the very center of the eye, you won't notice the eye swiveling because it will be looking straight out of the picture.

5b. If you draw the pupil at the "7 o'clock" position, rather than "3 o'clock," the eye will turn but it won't appear to follow the mouse-pointer.

5c. If the eye isn't centered correctly, the whole eye will revolve around the center point, not just the pupil—your poor pet will look very strange!

6.

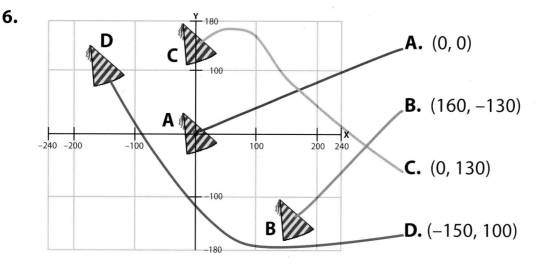

A. (0, 0)

B. (160, −130)

C. (0, 130)

D. (−150, 100)

7. The short script below would make the dog bark when he's clicked on.

You would have to load the sound "dog1" from the library

Build a similar script for your own pet sprite—there are lots of animal noises in the sound library. If your computer contains a microphone or you have one you can plug into it, why not record your own animal sounds? Just click on **Record new sound** (the microphone symbol) under the **Sounds** tab.

pages 31–34 Bounce Painting

1. Draw a line to link each pen block to its correct meaning.

pen down   Clear all pen drawing off the stage

pen up   Start drawing as the sprite moves

set pen size to ③   Stop drawing as the sprite moves

clear   Set how wide the pen line is

2. If you duplicated Ball2, the new sprite would be called **Ball3**.

3. If you put these two extra **go to** blocks between the **go to Ball2** and **pen up** blocks, the three balls would draw triangles.

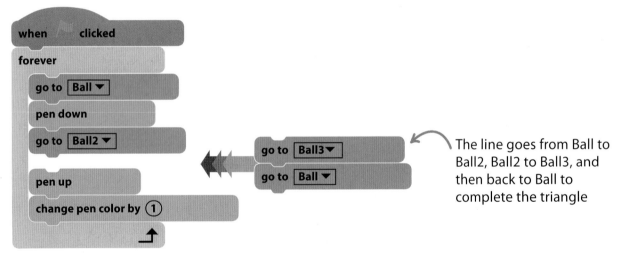

The line goes from Ball to Ball2, Ball2 to Ball3, and then back to Ball to complete the triangle

4. To get the lines to change color ten times quicker, change the 1 to a **10** in the **change pen color by** block.

5. If you add a **change shade by 10** pen block into the script below the **change pen color by** block, it changes the brightness as well as the color, so the picture becomes stripy.

6. If you check the check box of each ball's **Speed** variable, the names and speeds of both balls will show on the stage. You'll notice that they move at different speeds, because each ball has its own copy of the variable. Try it for yourself and see.

Getting Scratch

You can code online at the Scratch website, but if you aren't always connected to the Internet, you can install Scratch on your computer.

I always use a mouse!

Scratch is easier to use with a mouse than a touchpad

Online Scratch

If you sign up for an account on the Scratch website, you'll be able to save your projects online and share them with friends.

1 Before you sign up to Scratch, get permission from a parent with an email address. Go to **scratch.mit.edu** and select **Join Scratch**. You'll need to set up a username and password. Don't use your real name as your username.

2 Once you've joined the Scratch website, click **Sign in** and then enter your username and password. Click **Create** at the top of the screen to start a new project. Happy coding!

Scratch 2

Offline Scratch

When you don't have access to the Internet, or if you want to code offline, you'll need to download **Scratch 2.0** to your computer.

1 For the offline version of Scratch, go to **scratch.mit.edu/ scratch2download** and follow the installation instructions. The Scratch symbol will appear on your desktop.

2 To start Scratch, double-click on the **Scratch 2.0** symbol. When using Scratch offline, always save your work from time to time. (The online version saves automatically.)

Note for parents

The Scratch website is run by Massachusetts Institute of Technology (MIT). It is intended to be safe for children to use. The instructions in this book are for Scratch 2.0, not the older Scratch 1.4. The online version of Scratch works well on Windows, Mac, and Ubuntu computers; the offline version isn't compatible with all Ubuntu versions. At the time of writing, the Raspberry Pi can't run Scratch 2.0. Help your child work logically through any coding difficulties. Check for obvious errors, such as swapping similar blocks in scripts, and that scripts are controlling the correct sprites. Remember: coding should be fun!